FOOD

BRENDA WILLIAMS

RAINTREE
STECK-VAUGHN
PUBLISHERS
A Steck-Vaughn Company

Austin, Texas

ENVIRONMENT STARTS HERE

TITLES IN THE SERIES
Food · Recycling · Transportation · Water

Published by Raintree Steck-Vaughn Publishers, an imprint of Steck-Vaughn Company

Library of Congress Cataloging-in-Publication Data
Williams, Brenda.
Food / Brenda Williams.
    p.   cm.—(Environment starts here)
    Includes bibliographical references and index.
    Summary: Discusses the different kinds of food we eat, where they come from, and how they are preserved.
    ISBN 0-8172-5351-3
    1. Food—Juvenile literature.
    [1. Food.]
    I. Title. II. Series.
    TX355.W52 1999
    641.3—dc21   98-4586

Printed in Italy. Bound in the United States.
1 2 3 4 5 6 7 8 9 0 03 02 01 00 99

Picture Acknowledgments
Pages 1: Angela Hampton Family Life Pictures. 4: Eye Ubiquitous/David Cumming. 5: Frank Lane Picture Agency/Life Science Images. 6: Wayland Picture Library. 7, 9, 13, 15: Angela Hampton Family Life Pictures. 8: Eye Ubiquitous/Sue Passmore. 10: Eye Ubiquitous/Polypix. 12: Wayland Picture Library. 16-17: Tony Stone Images/Tony Craddock. 18: Tony Stone Images/Bruce Forster. 19: Topham Picturepoint. 20, 21: Wayland Picture Library. 23: Eye Ubiquitous/S. Miller. 24: Frank Lane Picture Agency/D. Dugan. 25, 28: Eye Ubiquitous/David Cumming. 27: Zefa Photo Library/Stockmarket. 29: Wayland Picture Library.
Cover: Zefa Photo Library/Streichan.
Illustrated by Rudi Vizi

The photo on page 1 shows a chef cutting up vegetables to prepare a meal.

CONTENTS

WHAT FOODS DO YOU EAT?   4
A Variety of Foods   6

FOOD FROM PLANTS   8
Helping Plants Grow   11
Organic Farming   13

FOOD FROM ANIMALS   14
Farming Methods   16
Food from the Sea   19

KEEPING FOOD FRESH   20
Preserving Food   22
Food Packaging   24

FOODS FROM FAR AWAY   26
Too Much or Too Little?   28

Glossary   30
Further Reading   31
Index   32

WHAT FOODS DO YOU EAT?

Food keeps you healthy and helps you grow. It gives your body the energy to work. Your food comes from plants and other animals.

Meat, fish, eggs, and cheese come from animals. Salads and vegetables, such as potatoes and peas, come from plants. So do nuts and fruits like apples and bananas.

This family is vegetarian. They eat eggs and dairy foods but no meat. Vegans are people who eat food only from plants.

Our bodies need all kinds of chemicals found in food. To stay healthy, we must eat a wide variety of foods like those shown here.

A Variety of Foods

Farmers grow plants and raise animals for meat to produce the food we buy.

Most of the food eaten in the world comes from plants. Our breakfast juice, cereals, and toast come from plants. Cereals are grass plants. Their seeds are called grains. Grains that are ground into flour are used to make bread and pasta such as spaghetti.

Your Daily Diet

Make a list of all the foods you eat on one day. Then make four headings: meat and fish, dairy food, grain, and fruits and vegetables. Put each of the foods you have eaten under the correct heading. This way you can find out what you eat most.

A selection of food made from plants, including grains of rice, bread, pasta, pastry, and cake

These girls are eating a healthy breakfast of cereal and milk, yogurt, fruit juice, toast, and eggs.

FOOD FROM PLANTS

Plants have leaves, stems, and roots. Many plants also produce flowers that develop into fruits. We eat all the different parts of plants and make some of them into juices to drink.

Vegetables such as cabbages are leaves. Potatoes are stems. Carrots and turnips are roots, and peas and beans are seeds. Nuts are seeds, too. All fruits have seeds in them.

Farmers use combine harvesters to gather cereals from fields and remove the grains.

Some farmers sell the fruit and vegetables they produce to people along roadsides.

Farmers use machines to spray crops with insect-killers, as here. Crops are any plants grown by farmers to sell.

Helping Plants Grow

Plants will die without plenty of water and sunlight. Farmers must water their crops if there is no rain every few days or weeks.

Farmers feed the soil with fertilizer to help plants grow big and strong. They also spray crops to keep insects from eating them or infecting them with germs. Some fertilizers and insect-killers are chemicals.

Cereal crops that are grown on fertilized soil produce bigger and fatter leaves and grains, as this comparison shows. Farmers use fertilizers to produce as much plant food as they can from their land.

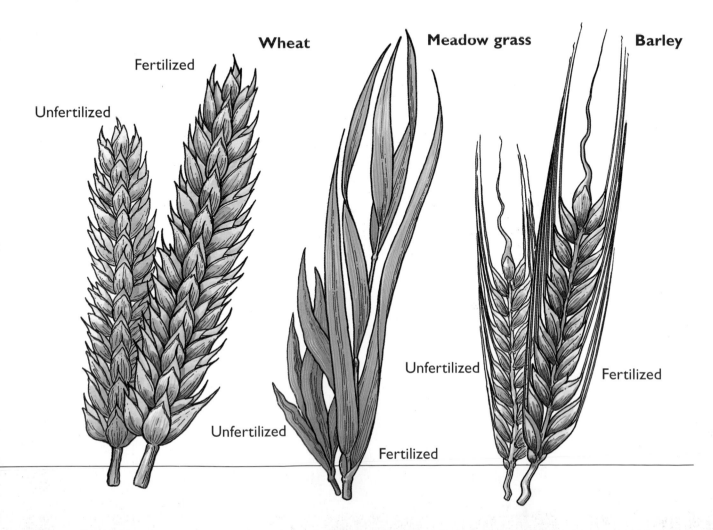

Wheat

Fertilized

Unfertilized

Unfertilized

Meadow grass

Unfertilized

Fertilized

Barley

Fertilized

Fruits are harvested, or taken from plants, when they are fully grown and juicy. This girl is picking strawberries.

Organic Farming

Farmers have machines to sow seeds, spread fertilizer, and spray plants. Chemical fertilizers and sprays make good crops, but they can also harm wild plants and animals.

Some farmers do not use chemicals. They grow organic, or naturally produced, crops. Their fertilizers and insect-killers come from plants and animal waste.

A family and friend eat fruits and drink tea and juice produced from organically grown plants.

FOOD FROM ANIMALS

Farmers keep animals for meat, milk, and eggs. The beef we eat comes from cows. We get lamb from sheep and pork from pigs. Meat is put into sausages, pies, burgers, or nuggets.

Cows and goats give the milk we drink. Milk is also made into dairy foods such as cheese, yogurt, and butter. Chickens lay the eggs we eat. They also provide meat, as do other birds like turkeys.

Milk from cows and goats goes to factories to be made into butter, cheese, yogurt, or cream. At the supermarket, look for other foods made from milk.

Milk

Ice-cream soda

Yogurt

Butter

Cheese

Ice cream

We can buy cuts of meat from the butcher or supermarket and cook them for dinner.

Farming Methods

Some farmers keep caged chickens in sheds. Others let "free-range" birds run around outside. The caged birds are "battery hens." They have no space to move and no light.

Some pigs and calves are also kept in sheds. They are fed chemicals to make them grow bigger and faster.

Cows graze in a field on farmland. It costs a farmer more to keep animals for food than to grow crops.

People around the world eat meat from many animals—cows, goats, sheep, pigs, ostriches, deer, guinea pigs, and various birds.

Compare Prices

A lot of people think "factory farming" is cruel. But it makes eggs and meat cheaper to buy. Next time you go shopping, compare the prices of battery and free-range eggs.

A selection of fish and shellfish to eat. River and sea life needs clean water to live in. We must keep rivers and seas free from pollution.

Food from the Sea

Nearly all the world's food comes from farms. Even some of the fish we eat comes from fish farms! Most fish, though, are caught in nets at sea.

We also eat shrimps, crabs, and other shellfish. In Asia, many people eat fish and shellfish as their main foods.

These boys have caught fish to eat from the sea off the coast of Western Australia.

KEEPING FOOD FRESH

Fresh food tastes best. Old milk smells and tastes sour. Old bread turns hard and moldy. Bad meat or fish stinks. Eating old or bad food can make you sick.

We keep some food cold in refrigerators to keep it from spoiling. Food from farms goes to factories and stores in refrigerated trucks.

Ideal foods to take on a picnic are sandwiches, pies, salads, fruit, and soft drinks. They will not spoil quickly if they are not refrigerated.

This girl is taking food from a refrigerator filled with fresh and prepared foods. The "sell by" date on food packages tells you if the food is still good to eat.

Preserving Food

Frozen food lasts for months. But we do not have to put all food into the refrigerator or freezer to preserve it or to keep it fresh.

Foods keep longer if they are heat treated, dried, salted, or pickled. Canned foods are heated first to kill any germs.

Most of the fruit and vegetables we eat are bought and eaten fresh. But carrots may be canned, corn can be frozen, fruit might be dried, and plums and peaches are often kept in a sweet syrup.

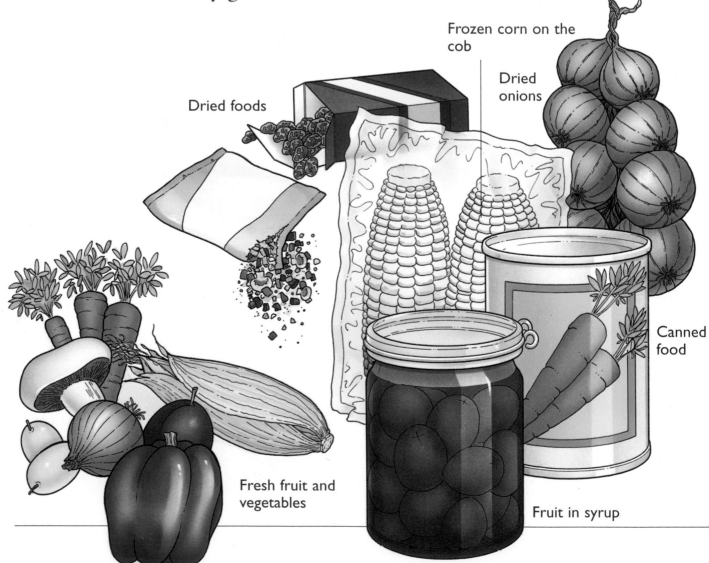

Dried foods

Frozen corn on the cob

Dried onions

Canned food

Fresh fruit and vegetables

Fruit in syrup

Packaged soups have been dried so only the solids remain. Fish may be salted, pickled in vinegar, or dried in smoke—like kippers. Meats like ham can be smoked, too.

In canning factories, prepared foods, like these cooked beets, are put into tin cans by machines. The cans are then sealed.

Food Packaging

A storekeeper may wrap up the bread, meat, or vegetables that you buy from a store.

Food in supermarkets often comes from a factory or is packed in plastic, paper, or cardboard. Drinks come in glass or plastic bottles and tin or aluminum cans.

Potatoes are picked from a field. Later they will be sold loose. Or they will be sealed in plastic bags to be sold in supermarkets.

Recycling

Save all the paper and packaging from food and drinks you use at home in one week. Then weigh it on the kitchen scales. You will find how much extra weight you carried home in your shopping bags.

Packaging adds to household waste. It uses up the world's scarce resources. We can help to save these by taking empty bottles and cans to a recycling center for reuse.

Supermarket packaging can be costly and may add to the price of some foods.

FOODS FROM FAR AWAY

Our food comes in ships, aircraft, and container trucks from all over the world. This is why we can buy fruit and vegetables grown in countries far away, where the weather is different.

We pay extra for the cost of bringing foods from abroad. Food will be cheaper if it is grown at home.

We can make a fruit salad with pineapples, bananas, oranges, mangoes, and other fruits grown around the world.

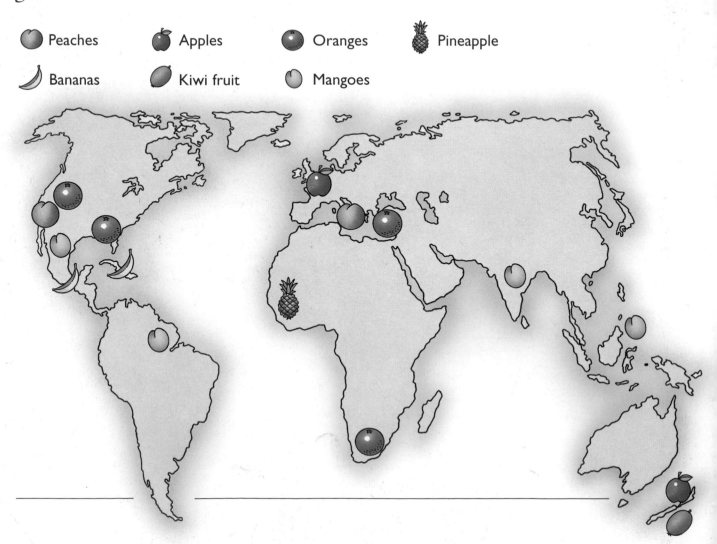

Peaches   Apples   Oranges   Pineapple

Bananas   Kiwi fruit   Mangoes

Boxes of strawberries grown in California are loaded onto a truck for shipment to Europe. Summer fruits like strawberries are now available all year round.

Too Much or Too Little?

People in rich countries often eat more food than their bodies need. In poor countries, many people go hungry and some die from lack of enough food and drink.

Some of us eat too many sugary foods like cakes. We often do not eat enough healthy foods such as fruit.

Farmers in these poor countries may grow crops of rice, beans, and corn all year round. They grow some to eat, and the rest they sell to countries whose people grow less food than they need.

Many ingredients, or food items, that we use to make meals come from distant countries, such as spices from India or China.

GLOSSARY

Cereal Grass plants such as wheat, oats, barley, rice, or corn.

Chemicals The "building bricks" of foods, substances, and materials. Foods include such chemicals as fats, sugars, proteins, and vitamins.

Crops Plants grown for sale by farmers.

Dairy foods Cream, cheese, yogurt, butter, and other foods made from milk.

Diet The mixture of foods a person eats. A "balanced" diet contains all the foods necessary to stay healthy.

Fertilizer Chemicals or natural plant food, such as animal dung and compost, used by farmers to make crops grow better.

Food Things we eat or drink that give us energy and help us grow and stay healthy.

Organic Grown in a natural way, without the use of chemicals.

Pasta Foods such as noodles and spaghetti made from wheat flour.

Recycling Using raw materials over and over again, instead of throwing them away.

Soil The earth in which plants grow.

Vegan A vegetarian who eats food only from plants

Vegetables Plant foods, which can be leaves, roots, stems, or fruits of plants.

Vegetarian Someone who does not eat meat but who drinks milk and eats the foods made from it.

FURTHER READING

Pulleyn, Micah and Sarah Bracken. *Kids in the Kitchen: Delicious, Fun, and Healthy Recipes to Cook and Bake.* New York: Sterling Publishing, Inc., 1995.

Tames, Richard. *Food: Feasts, Cooks, and Kitchens.* Danbury, CT: Franklin Watts, 1994.

Wolfe, Robert L. and Wolfe, Diane. *Vegetarian Cooking Around the World* (Easy Menu Ethnic Cookbooks). Minneapolis, MN: Lerner Group, 1992.

INDEX

Animals 4, 6, 12, 14, 16, 17

Battery hens 16
Beef 14
Bread 6, 20, 24
Butter 14

Cakes 6, 13, 28
Canned food 22, 23, 24
Cereals and grains 6, 7, 8, 30
Cheese 4, 14
Chemicals 5, 11, 12, 16, 30
Chickens 14, 16
Crops 10, 11, 12, 16, 29

Dairy foods 4, 6, 14, 30
Diet 30
Dried food 22, 23
Drinks 6, 7, 20, 24

Eggs 4, 7, 14, 17

Farms and farming 6, 8, 9, 10, 11, 12, 16, 17, 19, 20, 24, 29, 30
Fertilizers 10, 11, 12, 30
Fish 4, 6, 18, 19, 20, 23
Free-range 16
Fresh food 20, 21, 22, 23, 28
Frozen food 22
Fruit 4, 8, 9, 12, 13, 20, 21, 22, 26, 28

Health 4, 5, 7, 20, 28, 30

Lamb 14

Meat 4, 6, 14, 15, 16, 17, 20, 23, 24
Milk 7, 14, 20

Nuts 4, 8

Organic food 13, 31

Packaging 21, 24, 25
Pasta 6, 30
Pickled food 22, 23
Pies 14, 20
Plants 4, 6, 8, 10, 11, 12
Potatoes 8, 24
Preserving 22, 23

Refrigerator 20, 21, 22

Salads 4, 20
Salted food 22, 23
Sandwiches 20
Shellfish 18, 19

Vegetables 4, 8, 9, 22, 24, 26, 30